Copyright © 1988 Ideals Publishing Corporation
All rights reserved.
Printed and bound in the United States of America
Published by Ideals Publishing Corporation
Nelson Place at Elm Hill Pike
Nashville, Tennessee 37214

ISBN 0-8249-8343-2

A Child's Book of Prayers

By Pamela Kennedy

Illustrated by Katherine Wilson

IDEALS CHILDREN'S BOOKS

Nashville, Tennessee

O God, sometimes I wish I could give you a hug.
You're so big and strong, but still you care about
butterflies and baby birds and little kids like me.
I'm glad you're always there so I can talk to you
and tell you that I love you.

O Lord, I will sing praises to your name.

Psalm 18:49

I need you today, God.
I feel lonely and a little bit afraid.
I don't know anybody here.
And I don't have a friend.
But if you stay with me all day long,
I think things will be better.
And I won't need to feel so all alone.

Do not fear, for I am with you.

Isaiah 41:10

Thank you, God, for my food—
for oatmeal that makes my tummy warm on
winter mornings and for watermelon and
lemonade on hot summer days.
I'm so glad you give me good things to eat.

Let us be thankful and so worship God.

Hebrews 12:28

Jesus, sometimes it's hard to be little.
I forget to do the things I'm told,
and then I get into trouble.
Do you remember what it's like to be small?
Would you help me be good today?

Children, obey your parents in everything for this pleases the Lord.
Colossians 3:20

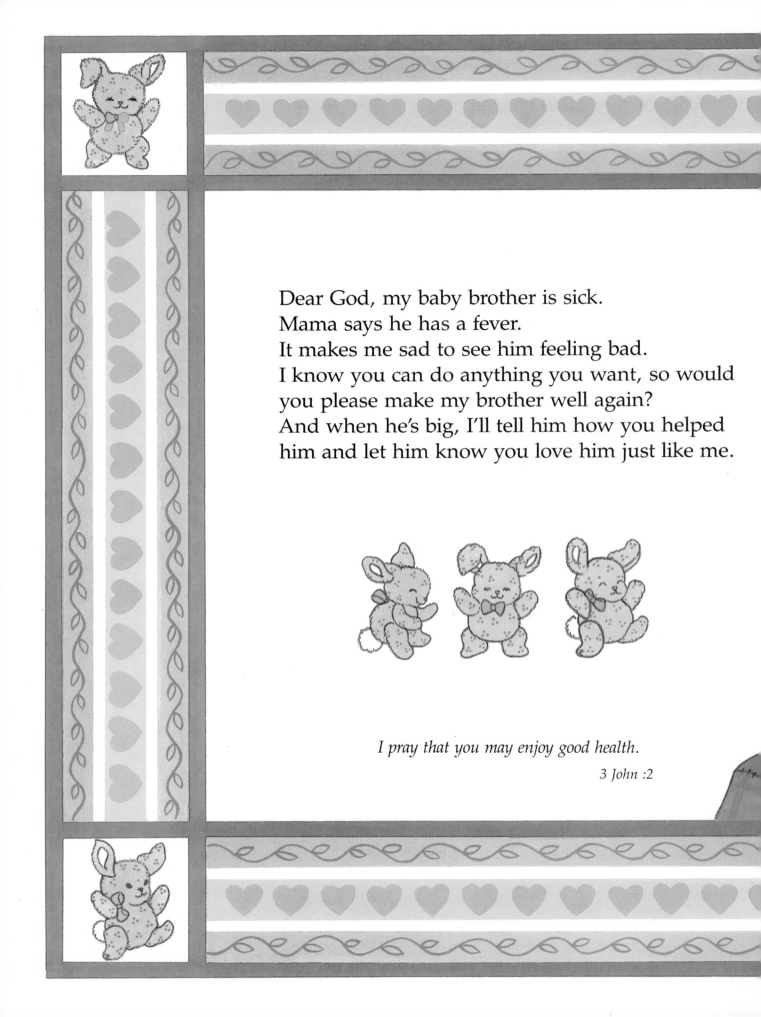

Dear God, my baby brother is sick.
Mama says he has a fever.
It makes me sad to see him feeling bad.
I know you can do anything you want, so would you please make my brother well again?
And when he's big, I'll tell him how you helped him and let him know you love him just like me.

I pray that you may enjoy good health.

3 John :2

Dear God, I saw a crocus today and that means
spring is here!
I love it when you make the world all green again
and birds have babies
and the rain makes splashy puddles.
Thank you for a world of brand new things.

Flowers appear on the earth; the season of singing has come.

Song of Solomon 2:12

Thank you, God, for the summer.
I love to feel the warm sun and smell the flowers
and play in the sand at the beach.
When the trees all wave at heaven, does summer
make you happy, too?

You made both summer and winter.

Psalm 74:17b

Did you see the trees today, God?
They are all yellow and red and gold.
The gray squirrels are busy gathering nuts,
and the pumpkins are ready to pick.
Thank you for crispy leaves and crunchy apples
and for painting the world with colors every fall.

He has made everything beautiful in its time.

Ecclesiastes 3:11

Dear God, thank you for winter when the world sleeps under a blanket of snow.
Icicles drip in the sun, and my snowman smiles in the yard.
And thank you, too, for a cozy house where I can be snug and warm.

There is a time for everything and a season for every activity under heaven.

Ecclesiastes 3:1

Dear God, today I had a bad day.
On the way to school I pushed my friend; then I didn't want to share the swings.
I got mad at my sister and called her names.
And now I feel just awful.
Could you help me start all over, God?
And tomorrow I'll try harder to be good.

You are kind and forgiving, O Lord.

Psalm 86:5

I'm glad you gave me parents, God,
because they help me in doing so many things—
like throwing balls and catching fish and making
bread and flying kites.
But mostly they are good for hugging tight
and making all the bad times go away.

Honor your father and your mother.

Deuteronomy 5:16

Jesus, will you stay beside my bed?
It's dark at night and lonely, too, when creaky sounds and shadows are around.
But you are not afraid because you made the darkness.
So if you are with me, I will be all right.

When I am afraid, I will trust in you.

Psalm 56:3

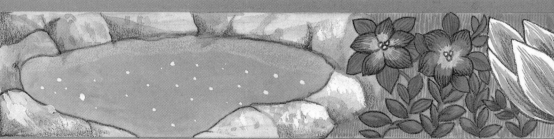